Swan Lake

STORIES OF THE BALLETS

Swan Lake

Ann Nugent

BARRON'S

Woodbury, N.Y. • London • Toronto • Sydney

Also in this series:
THE NUTCRACKER
PETRUSHKA
GISELLE

First published in Great Britain 1985
by Aurum Press Ltd.

First U.S. Edition 1985 by Barron's Educational Series,
Inc.

This book has been
produced by Aurum Press
Ltd., 33 Museum Street,
London WC1A 1LD.

Edited and illustrated by
E.T. Archive Ltd, 15 Lots Road, London SW10 0QH.

Designed by Julian Holland

All inquiries should be addressed to:
Barron's Educational Series, Inc.
113 Crossways Park Drive
Woodbury, New York 11797

Library of Congress Catalog Card No. 85-15019
International Standard Book No. 0-8120-5674-4

Printed in Belgium
567   9 8 7 6 5 4 3 2 1

Front cover: Merle Park and Anthony Dowel in *Swan Lake*.
Royal Ballet, 1977 (Reg Wilson)
Back cover: Design for Prince Siegfried by Leslie Hurry
(Royal Benevolent Fund)
Endpapers: Design for the ballroom scene in Act III by
Leslie Hurry (Royal Ballet Benevolent Fund)
Title-page: The swans in Act II. Royal Ballet, 1977 (Reg Wilson)
Half-title: Margot Fonteyn and Robert Helpman. Royal Ballet, 1943
(Theatre Museum)

Contents

The Plot **6**
The Libretto and Score **12**
The First Performance, 1877 **16**
The 1895 Production **20**
Tchaikovsky **24**
The Nineteenth Century **30**
The Twentieth Century **40**
Index and Acknowledgments **48**

Ann Nugent trained at the Arts Educational Schools,
specializing in ballet, and danced with the London Festival
Ballet for seven years. She is now dance critic for
The Stage and a regular contributor to *Dance and Dancers*;
she also collaborated with Craig Dodd on the book
An Introduction to Ballet.

The Plot

The story of the ballet Swan Lake has been subjected to endless modifications and adaptations. For simplification this scenario is based on the Royal Ballet's most recent production in 1979 since it is directly descended from the original Petipa/Ivanov version given in St Petersburg in 1895.

From the first notes of his overture Tchaikovsky warns us that *Swan Lake* is going to be a haunting, mysterious and highly charged emotional experience. Straight away we are alerted to the sadness of the swan theme played first with plaintive melancholy by the oboe, then echoed by the clarinet and filled out on the strings and woodwind. Soon the music grows ominous and threatening as it surges and accelerates to a dark climax, emphasized by loud crashing sounds on the brass, followed immediately by the swan theme now expanded into full orchestral colour. We know then that this is to be tragedy on a grand scale, a story of romantic love condemned by forces of evil.

Act I

As the curtain rises, however, the music is hastening along in rejoicing mood, and peasants are merrily gathering for a birthday party. We have stepped back in time to the Middle Ages, to the grounds of a great castle in Germany where celebrations are beginning for Prince Siegfried's coming of age. As he arrives, courtiers and friends entertain him with a sparkling waltz. The Queen Mother enters and is perturbed at the signs of so much revelry, for she has a serious matter to discuss with her son and tells him that it is high time he married. It is her wish that he select a bride at the ball she has arranged for him the following day.

Marriage is not something he wants to think about yet, and when his mother has departed he puts her command out of his mind and, fingering the ornate crossbow she has given to him, settles down to watch the entertainment. Three friends dance a spirited *pas de trois* and afterwards he watches with considerable amusement as his old tutor Wolfgang, who is thoroughly intoxicated, picks out a peasant girl and tries to teach her a court dance. But she gets the better of him, sends him spinning into the arms of the laughing crowd, and delightedly finishes the dance on her own.

As the party is drawing to a close, the Prince invites all the peasants to join together in a brisk *polacca*, with much clapping of hands, stamping and swirling of bright ribbons. It ends with cheerful waves to the host and a general exodus.

Right
The setting for Act I, Scene 2 (more familiar as Act II), designed by Bocharov for the 1895 production at the Maryinsky Theatre, St Petersburg

Below
Act I of Jack Carter's production for London Festival Ballet, with Ben Stevenson as Prince Siegfried and Niels Kehlet as the Jester

Glad to be alone at last, Siegfried reveals that he is in melancholy mood, yearning for something unattainable: doubtless an idealized love. But a flock of swans flying in the distance interrupts his reflections and, picking up his crossbow, he goes off in search of them.

Act II

At a clearing in the forest by the lakeside Baron von Rothbart (the name means red beard) sits, brooding, in the guise of a malevolent owl; at the sound of the Prince's party he hurries away. Siegfried dismisses the friends who have joined him, indicating that he prefers to hunt alone. He sees a swan approaching and picks up his crossbow, but to his astonishment the creature turns into a beautiful young woman. It is Odette who, frightened, begs the Prince not to shoot, and tells him that she and her companions have been captured by the wicked magician von Rothbart, and turned into swans. They swim on the lake which has been formed from a pool of her mother's tears, shed at her daughter's plight, but between midnight and dawn they are able to return to their human form. They can only be saved if a man who has never before committed himself to a woman makes her a promise of undying love. At this moment, von Rothbart reappears and Siegfried seizes his crossbow, but once again Odette pleads with him not to shoot, for the death of this man would end all chances of release from the spell.

The two withdraw and swan maidens (as stylized swans) cross the stage in weaving lines and changing patterns, ending in a group which Odette, in her protective role as the Swan Queen, rushes in to lead. The swans then dance a waltz, which is followed by the great central *pas de deux* for Odette and Siegfried, an adagio of lyric beauty, in which the two declare their growing love.

After such intensity four cygnets provide a moment of relief as, with linked arms, they present the celebrated Dance of the Little Swans. Odette reappears in a solo of deep melancholy, and there is further dancing from two Big Swans, then from all the swans, reaching a climax as the Prince lifts his Queen high above his head *en attitude*. But dawn is approaching, and although Siegfried tries to restrain Odette, von Rothbart's power forces her and her companions to leave and to return to the lake as swans.

Act III

It is early evening the following day, and under the

Maya Plisetskaya and Nikolai Fadeyechev in the great white adagio of Act II with the Bolshoi Ballet. The surrounding group of swans

welcoming eye of the Master of Ceremonies courtiers and guests are gathering for the Prince's birthday ball. His mother expects him to choose a bride from among six princesses whom she has invited and, after watching a crystalline *pas de quatre*, she asks him to dance with them. But although each is charming and elegant, he causes offence by declining to offer his hand to any one of them. Clearly his

adds to the feeling of sadness, and the dancers' proud lines emphasize the pedigree of the Russian school of ballet

mind is on Odette. The ball, however, must go on and the celebrations continue with a jubilant display of national dances—from Spain (bolero), Hungary (czardas), Naples (tarantella) and Poland (mazurka).

Suddenly a fanfare announces the arrival of von Rothbart and Odile, his daughter, dressed in black and identical in appearance to Odette. The Prince is captivated, and together they dance a virtuoso showpiece, the Black Swan *pas de deux*. Convinced that this brilliant and glamorous woman is his true love, and oblivious of Odette who appears in anguish at a window, Siegfried asks for her hand in marriage (it is one of ballet's anomalies that he cannot see the impossibility of his gentle Odette ever transforming into such a temptress). At von Rothbart's insistence Siegfried swears eternal allegiance, but as he does so the scene darkens, and resounding chords from the brass announce the victory of von Rothbart and his daughter. They depart in triumph, knowing that Odette is now trapped forever by the spell and the Prince, realizing his tragic mistake, rushes off to find her.

Watercolour depicting von Rothbart by Leslie Hurry, who first designed a production for the Royal Ballet in 1943. His revised designs were used for subsequent productions in 1952, 1965 and for the touring company in 1979

Act IV

At another clearing by the lake, the swan maidens await their queen. In deepest distress Odette returns to them, and tries to drown herself in the lake. Gently her companions restrain her. Meanwhile von Rothbart, gloating, whips up a storm, but Siegfried, utterly distraught at what he has done, will not let this prevent him from finding Odette and imploring her forgiveness. Sad but resigned, she does forgive him, but both are doomed and, with the approaching dawn, realize that there is only one course open to them: they must die together. In vain von Rothbart tries to prevent them, but Odette throws herself into the lake, followed by Siegfried. Their sacrifice, however, has destroyed von Rothbart's power, and he too dies.

Apotheosis

As dawn breaks the swans line up diagonally across the stage to pay homage to their Queen, and Odette and Siegfried are seen drifting away on a golden barque to a visionary land where their love may remain eternal.

The Libretto and Score

No one knows exactly how *Swan Lake* was conceived for while historians over the years have uncovered many clues some of its origins will now always remain obscure. Long before the first performance in Moscow in 1877, Tchaikovsky was probably mulling over ideas for such a ballet, since in 1871 during a summer holiday at Kamenka, the Ukrainian home of his sister and her family, he had composed a modest little ballet to amuse her children, calling it *The Lake of Swans*. Details of that event are sketchy but, according to Soviet ballet historian Yuri Slonimsky, Tchaikovsky's niece, Anna Meck-Davydov, spoke of it. At the time she would have been seven (although her memory puts the year back to 1867), and she claimed that, 'My sister participated; she was six. My Uncle Modeste Ilyich [the composer's younger brother] performed the role of the prince. I represented Cupid . . . The magnificent wooden swans on which we rocked were in the house for a long time.'

Tchaikovsky's nephew Yuri Lvovich Davydov also referred to the ballet, though since he was not born until 1876 his version is based on hearsay. He pointed out in his *Memoirs about P.I. Tchaikovsky* that, although most of the children's entertainment would not have been recognized at the ballet's première, 'the principal theme, "The Song of the Swans", was then the same as now'. He was probably referring to the music that occurs at the end of Act I, when harp arpeggios and tremolo strings introduce a new swan leitmotiv.

Tchaikovsky perhaps pursued the idea during regular discussions he held with a group of friends who were intent on the development of the arts in Moscow. In any event, the idea of the swan as a symbol of womanhood at its purest is ancient. Cyril Beaumont pointed out in his book *The Ballet Called Swan Lake* that, 'The myth of the Swan-Maiden is one of the oldest and most beautiful legends in the world, and it reappears in slightly different forms in the literatures of almost all countries, both Occidental and Oriental', adding that, 'The episode of the huntsman about to shoot a swan which changes into a beautiful maiden is to be found in both Russian and South German folk lore.'

Such legends were presumably familiar to Tchaikovsky and his friends, and it is possible that, when they gathered in the club-like atmosphere of the Artistic Circle or the Shilovskaya Salon, they began to explore ideas about transforming them into a ballet. It is also possible that a story alluding to a lake of swans, in an eighteenth-century collection of fairy-tales by Johann Musäus, had some

Tchaikovsky's beloved sister Alexandra and her husband Lev Davidov, surrounded by their children: standing at back Tatyana and Natalya, seated on either side of their parents, Vera and Anna, and in front Vladimir (Bob), Yury and Dimitry. Bob was to become a close confidant of the composer

influence on the libretto which eventually came to be written in 1876 by two men, Vladimir Petrovich Begichev and Vasily Fedorovich Geltser. It is difficult to say for certain how much each contributed to the work, or even whether Geltser (a dancer with the Moscow company who later became *régisseur*) was more than just a copyist.

It was Begichev, however, as Intendant of the Moscow Imperial Theatres, who commissioned Tchaikovsky in May 1875 to write the score of *Swan Lake*. Tchaikovsky was a close family friend who, seven years earlier, had accompanied Begichev and his stepson, Vladimir Shilovsky (a favourite pupil of Tchaikovsky's), on a tour of western Europe, including a trip down the Rhine with its magical castles, which may have sown the seeds of *Swan Lake*.

Hans Christian Andersen wrote a fairy-tale about swans markedly different from the swan-maiden legend. In The Wild Swans it was men who were metamorphosed into swans rather than women. Eleven handsome princes, at the whim of their wicked stepmother, had to become swans by night. The story had a happy ending for eventually their beautiful young sister, Elise, discovered their plight and, at great personal cost, was able to restore them to permanent manhood

Begichev's wife, the former widow Marya Vasilevna Shilovskaya, assembled the progressive artists at her intimate soirées; her elder son Konstantin was later to collaborate with the composer on the libretto for *Eugène Onegin*.

Tchaikovsky at the time of his commission had no practical knowledge of the specialist medium of composing for dance, though like all well-to-do men of his day he was in the habit of going to plays, operas and ballets. In 1870 he had occupied himself with large-scale ideas about writing a four-act ballet *Cinderella*, though he seems to have abandoned them fairly quickly, leaving no trace of any music he may have written for it. Now with *Swan Lake* in train he began to immerse himself in the technical requirements of ballet music and pored over scores borrowed from the Moscow theatre library.

The quality of ballet music then was rather poor, a factor due in part perhaps to the stifling atmosphere of imperial bureaucracy, and to the strictures imposed on official ballet composers. Tchaikovsky was not bound by any rule of office, but in the event he had a far richer imagination, as had been revealed in a blossoming career which by then (he was thirty-five in May 1875) had produced four operas, two symphonies, one piano concerto, two string quartets, and various other incidental works.

Left
Tower and Mill, Andernach
on the Rhine, *watercolour
by Clarkson Stanfield
(1793–1867). A journey
down the Rhine made in
1868 by Tchaikovsky and
the Intendant of the Imperial
Theatres, may have sown
the seeds for* Swan Lake

He responded to the *Swan Lake* initiative with fervour, and in August made a telling and much quoted remark in a letter to the composer Rimsky-Korsakov: 'I took on this work partly for the money, which I need, and partly because I have long wanted to try my hand at this kind of music'.

The completed score was ready by April 1876 when doubtless he heaved a sigh of relief. Only a month earlier he had written to his brother Anatoli: 'I am up to my eyes in the orchestration of my ballet which must be ready by St Thomas's week. As I still have to finish two and a half acts I have decided to work at this most boring task both in Holy and Easter Weeks; to be able to do this I must get away from here.' He went to spend two weeks in the country with Vladimir Shilovsky, but seems to have written *Swan Lake* mostly in his Moscow home (in between composing one or two other works, writing critical articles *and* teaching at the Conservatoire), and during holidays at his sister's family home, Kamenka. Travels in Europe alerted him to the music of other contemporary composers, and Wagner's *Lohengrin* may have had some influence. But after hearing Delibe's *Sylvia* he wrote: 'If I had known this music earlier I would not have written *Swan Lake*, for it is poor stuff compared to *Sylvia*'.

Above
Wagner's Lohengrin *drawn by Wilhelm Karlbach, from his* Scenes from Famous Operas, 1877, was *a favourite opera of Tchaikovsky's. Once again the swan is a symbol of innocence and purity*

The First Performance, 1877

Rehearsals at the Bolshoi Theatre in Moscow for the first performance went on for an incredible eleven months. They had begun before Tchaikovsky finished the score, and in March 1876 he wrote to Modeste: 'If you could have seen how comical the ballet master looked, composing the dances in a most serious and concentrated manner, to the accompaniment of a little fiddle. At the same time it was a pleasure to watch the male and female dancers smiling at the future audience and looking forward to the possibility of jumping, pirouetting and turning about in the execution of their holy duty. Everybody in the theatre is delighted with my music!'

But they were not always so delighted with his music which, in its emotional and structural content, was so far in advance of anything experienced before in ballet that accusations of 'undanceable' were soon levelled at it. Unaccustomed to working with composers of stature, let alone genius, the company did not know how to relate to music that, far from merely providing support, actually led the way with its melodic and psychological development into a fantasy that could also be seen in terms of an allegory about unattainable love. Lack of understanding seems to have led to contemptuous treatment of the score, and the orchestra, under a conductor who may or may not have merited the description 'semi-amateur', thought it altogether too complex and difficult.

Without doubt one of the main problems was that the choreography was entrusted to a mediocre choreographer. Julius Reisinger (1827-92) was an Austrian whose sole claim to fame today is his failure with *Swan Lake*. Critics observed that 'Mr Reisinger's dances are weak in the extreme . . . Incoherent waving of the legs that continued through the course of four hours—is this not torture? The *corps de ballet* stamp up and down in the same place, waving their arms like a windmill's vanes—and the soloists jump about the stage in gymnastic steps.'

Moreover, the designs lacked coherence, for they were conceived by three different men. Acts I and III were by two décor painters, a Mr Shangin and a Mr Gropius, whose contributions have long since vanished. Acts II and IV, however, were by Karl Valts, a stage machinist, and two engravings exist, which do at least suggest that a strange and intriguing fantasy was created on stage, though we cannot be certain how accurately they depict his work.

Ballet companies then, as now, had good and bad phases, and the Moscow company was going through an undistinguished period, lacking a ballet-master with the creative

Right
Two engravings from the 1877 production, showing Karl Valts' designs for Acts II and IV. These are the only pictorial documents of their kind which survive from the original Moscow ballet

Above
Anna Sobeshchanskaya (1842–1918) as Odette in the original 1877 production. She was the leading Moscow ballerina of her day, but did not appear in the role until the fourth performance

drive that is the life-blood of ballet. Ironically, the role of Odette went to the less talented of two leading women, Pelagia Mikhailovna Karpakova, to whom the première was unexpectedly given as a benefit performance. There have been suggestions that it was a political move, since the superior dancer Anna Iosifovna Sobeshchanskaya had offended the Governor-General of Moscow by accepting presents of jewels from him, then marrying Stanislav Gillert who promptly sold the jewels. Gillert was himself a dancer, not notably gifted, but he nonetheless was given the part of Siegfried.

We do not know whether in those early days the same dancer also appeared as Odette and Odile (a tradition established in 1895 by Petipa and Ivanov), as the first cast list shows only three asterisks where her name should appear. The asterisks could have denoted duplication, on the other hand the role may have gone to another dancer.

By the ballet's fourth performance Sobeshchanskaya was permitted to dance Odette but, realizing in advance that the scope of the role was limited, she took herself off to St Petersburg and persuaded Petipa to create an additional *pas de deux* for herself and her partner (again Gillert). Perhaps she was feeling vulnerable at the time, for it was generally

The pas de trois *in Act I of Jack Carter's production for London Festival Ballet. The designs are by John Truscott*

agreed that while she had merited the title 'ballerina' (a distinction that can by no means be accorded to every woman appearing in leading roles) at thirty-four she was past her prime. Tchaikovsky was appalled when he discovered that she intended to dance her new *pas de deux*, which had music by Ludwig Minkus, in the third act of his ballet. But after long discussions he did agree that he would write additional music for her at top speed, basing it 'bar for bar, note for note' on the Minkus music, so that the choreography could be retained.

The original *Swan Lake* seemed doomed by its contributory elements, and for years afterwards it was simply dismissed as a failure. Nonetheless, Roland John Wiley in his book *Tchaikovsky's Ballets* argues that it may not have been quite such a disaster: 'At a time when new ballets normally received no more than eighteen performances Swan Lake's Moscow run of forty-one performances and of three productions in six years, is proof of the ballet's success and the interest it created'. Another Moscow ballet master, Joseph Hansen from Belgium, made further productions in 1880 and 1882. In 1884 he also produced another rather curious version in London called *The Swans*, with music written by Georges Jacobi.

Act IV of the Royal Ballet's production in 1971, using choreography by Ivanov, with Deanne Bergsma as the betrayed Odette

The 1895 Production

If Tchaikovsky was the architect of *Swan Lake*, its master builders did not emerge until two years after his death when, in 1895, Marius Petipa and Lev Ivanov choreographed a new production at the Maryinsky Theatre in St Petersburg (now renamed the Kirov Theatre in Leningrad). Petipa as ballet master was by then steeped in Tchaikovsky's music for the two had worked together in 1890 on *The Sleeping Beauty*, followed by *The Nutcracker* in 1892, which Petipa had planned, but was forced by illness to hand over the choreography to Ivanov.

Their collaboration was engineered by Ivan Alexandrovich Vsevolojsky, director of the Imperial Theatres in St Petersburg from 1881 to 1899. He was a cultured man of wisdom and vision who made sweeping reforms in the organization of the theatres, ensuring that ballet training was codified, that the post of official composer was abolished and that productions should come together as a more homogeneous entity. He conceived the idea of a ballet based on Perrault's fairy-tales, and by selecting Tchaikovsky to create the music and Petipa the choreography for *The Sleeping Beauty*, secured one of the finest partnerships in the entire history of ballet.

There is dissent over who subsequently took the initiative with *Swan Lake*. Petipa seems to have been convinced that there must have been something from the 1877 version worth salvaging, for he said in his *Memoirs*: 'I could not assume that Tchaikovsky's music was bad, that his part of the work had no success; the problem was not in the music but in the production of the ballet, in the dances'.

So the score was acquired; but the first that the St Petersburg public saw of the ballet was at a memorial concert for the composer in 1893 which included the first lakeside scene. Choreography was by Ivanov, since Petipa was reported to have been too busy to attend to it. Possibly his work load was precautionary after the ballet's earlier reception, but whatever his reasoning he saw that his assistant had responded well nigh perfectly to the music's call, and the scene (later called Act I, Scene 2, instead of its more usual listing as Act II) remained unaltered in the complete production. Petipa further assigned the choreography for the closing lakeside scene to Ivanov, while he undertook Acts I and II with some help from Ivanov. The programme credited Petipa alone, and it was not until long after the Russian Revolution that Ivanov's contribution was acknowledged.

Considerable revision was made to the libretto, first by Modeste Tchaikovsky and then by editors at the Maryinsky.

Pierina Legnani (1863–1923) as Odette in the 1894 memorial concert for Tchaikovsky. Italian born, she was the leading virtuoso dancer of her day, and created the role of Odette/Odile in the 1895 St Petersburg production, after which one critic observed that she was 'the supreme ideal of plastic movement'. She is remembered chiefly for the thirty-two fouettés she introduced into the Black Swan pas de deux. She had first executed them in London in a production of Aladdin *at the Alhambra Theatre in 1892.*

The score too was cut, modified, and significantly re-orchestrated by the conductor Riccardo Drigo who, conscious of the responsibility vested in him, wrote: 'It was my lot, like a surgeon, to perform an operation on *Swan Lake*, and I feared that I might not grasp the individuality of the great Russian master'. Wiley proposes that Drigo's alter-

Cartoon of Legnani by Nicholas Legat (1869– 1937). Legat was a premier danseur at St Petersburg and later became a famous teacher

Above
Act II, London Festival Ballet. Carter's most notable change to the original score in this act was an extension of the celebrated pas de deux, *so that it gained an allegro coda instead of the familiar melancholic ending*
Left
Pavel Gerdt (1844–1917), who created the leading man's role in all three of Tchaikovsky's ballets at St Petersburg
Right
The apotheosis for the Maryinsky Theatre

ations made more dramatic and theatrical sense, but points out that 'he damaged Tchaikovsky's subtle tonal plan'.

Pierina Legnani, an Italian, took the dual role of Odette/ Odile and by all accounts tempered her natural virtuosity to respond to the poetic ideal of Odette. She is especially remembered, however, for introducing, shortly after the première, the celebrated *fouettés* into the Black Swan *pas de deux*, in which Odile makes thirty-two *relevé* turns on one leg, whipped around by her 'working' leg. The part of Siegfried was taken by Pavel Gerdt, who may once have had the characteristics of the *danseur noble* but who was fifty by then, and a little beyond enacting a 21-year-old prince. Presumably his strength was also on the wane, which is perhaps why Siegfried's friend Benno was allotted some of the more strenuous partnering.

27 January 1895 (Julian Calendar) was the date of the production's first performance, and one critic summed it up as lavish: 'The settings of the second act by M. Levogt are very beautiful, that for the last act, the swan lake is by M. Bocharov. The apotheosis is likewise lovely. The music of the ballet is very melodious, but it contains an excess of waltzes.' Another critic wrote, 'What a poetical ballet is *Swan Lake* . . . what a beautiful white swan is Mlle Legnani', and yet a third said, 'M.I. Petipa distinguished himself wonderfully well in the production'.

Generally speaking the music was undervalued and dismissed as inadequate. But this was to be the production that gave the legend of greatness to *Swan Lake*.

Tchaikovsky

Peter Ilyich Tchaikovsky was essentially a symphonic composer, but writing for his three ballets touched on something in his heart, so that the music flowed inexorably. His gift of embroidering melody and repeating themes made it a never-ending source of fresh discovery.

Swan Lake is perhaps the most personal of his ballets, rich as it is in orchestral texture, contour and interwoven with feelings and passions. Some of the early reviewers, however, were downright scathing about the score, complaining that it was 'pallid and monotonous in the extreme'. A few did acknowledge, grudgingly, that it had some virtues. But perhaps the most telling observation came from Herman Avgustovich Laroche, the celebrated critic who had studied with Tchaikovsky at the Conservatoire, and who first saw the ballet eighteen months after its première. He wrote that

Above
Peter Ilyich Tchaikovsky, born in May 1840 at Votinsk on the borders of the Vyatka Province. Shortly before his death in November 1893 in St Petersburg his Sixth Symphony received its first performance. He believed it to be his best work. His brother, Modeste, gave it the title 'Pathetic' which for the Russian embodied feelings of passion, emotion and suffering, and is perhaps symbolic of the composer's life

... *the melodies, one more plastic than the last, more harmonious and captivating, flow as from a horn of plenty; the rhythm of the waltz, which prevails among the danced numbers, is embodied in such varied, graceful and winning designs that never did the melodic invention of the gifted, many-faceted composer stand the test more resplendently ... His music is ballet music completely, but at the same time really excellent and interesting for the serious musician. Frequently after a light dance motive, transparently harmonised and which serves as material for the first 'figure' of some dance, the symphonist in the composer awakens, and on the second figure illuminates us with the succession of thick and rich chords, which for a long time remind you of that strength, not of the ballet manner that he holds in check.*

Tchaikovsky's head was filled with music, unlikely as it may seem for the son of the chief inspector of the mines and metallurgical works at Votinsk, where he was born in 1840. He was the second of six children (with an older step-sister, born to his father's first wife, who had died in 1831) and grew up in a comfortable and prosperous home. His father was hard-working if unimaginative, while his mother, who came of French ancestry, was both artistic and creative, with a gift for languages and piano. Doubtless it is through her that Tchaikovsky inherited his gifts: also his nervous temperament. She died suddenly, of cholera, when he was only fourteen. It was a trauma that left an irreparable scar in him. It seems to have intensified his debilitating nervous disorders and left him with a craving for maternal solicitude. Who can say whether it contributed to his homosexuality, a factor that clearly influenced his later creative work. Music alone could provide him with solace and, while he had come late to

Right
Mozart's opera Don Giovanni *proved a turning point in Tchaikovsky's life, for it was after a performance in 1850 that he decided to devote his life to music*

serious musical studies, a month after the death of his mother
he began his first attempts at composition.

His French governess (and lifelong friend) Fanny Durbach
had already discerned a creative talent in him when she
joined the household in 1844 and, aware of his acute
sensitivity and high intelligence she used to refer to him as 'a
porcelain child'. She once found him sitting up in bed
crying, 'Oh this music, this music! Take it away! It's in here
(striking his forehead) and it won't let me sleep.' Early music
from the family's orchestrion (a type of mechanical organ),
largely excerpts from the operas of Rossini, Donizetti and
Bellini, charmed him. Then when he was about ten he was
taken to a performance of *Don Giovanni* which so over-
whelmed him that he decided from henceforth his life had to
be devoted to music.

Nevertheless, after his mother's death he was enrolled at
the School of Law in St Petersburg which, on his graduation,
gave him a serving rank in the Justice Department. He was to
make only moderate advances from there, for his heart was
elsewhere, and soon he began to study music theory through
the Russian Musical Society.

In 1862 the Society founded the St Petersburg Conservatoire, and Tchaikovsky became one of its first students.
Music began to absorb him more and more and by the
second year he had progressed to the class of the pianist and
composer Anton Rubinstein. Gradually he turned away from
friends who had no musical interests, and changed from a
dandified young man to one who went about looking
threadbare and unkempt. Soon he resigned from the Ministry
of Justice to concentrate full time on his studies, trying at the
same time to earn a meagre living from teaching and
accompanying at concerts. It was the start of trying financial
times which were not to be eased until the patroness,
Nadezhda von Meck, recognizing a rare talent, began
subsidizing his work in 1876. Although they were never to
meet properly, she helped him for many years.

After graduating from the Conservatoire he obtained a
teaching post at the newly established Moscow Conservatoire, and so began years of intensive work when he taught
and worked as a music critic in order to finance his
composing. His creations usually attracted mixed critical
response, though when they were still students Laroche told
him: 'Frankly I consider you to possess the greatest talent in
contemporary Russia. In you I see the greatest, indeed the
only hope for our musical future.' Not long afterwards there
was a two-year silence between the two after Laroche had
criticized Tchaikovsky's first opera *The Voyevoda*, claiming

*An artist's impression of St
Petersburg in 1812, with the
Grand Theatre on the left*

that the composer was 'too strongly influenced by Schumann's disciples, that his style wobbled between German and Italian styles and that it was insufficiently Russian'. Tchaikovsky later used music from *The Voyevoda* for the Act IV entr'acte of *Swan Lake*. He also salvaged the closing duet from his second opera *Undine*, which was never performed and which he eventually burnt, turning it into the ballet's central Act II *pas de deux*.

In 1877 he entered into a disastrous marriage almost as if fate, to which he often referred, had ordained it. The pain and anguish caused by this relationship was reflected both in his health and in his music. Eventually his family came to the rescue and a permanent separation was arranged.

*Tchaikovsky's manuscript
showing the swan theme*

His mature years fell into a pattern of prolific composition, into which he poured both worry, particularly about money and his inadequacies, and inspiration. At his death, in addition to the three ballets, he had written six major symphonies, eleven operas, three concertos for piano, and one for violin, numerous symphonic poems, suites, songs and many works for piano and chamber ensembles.

He enjoyed good food and travel, and despaired when the weather or his health were bad. He was a prolific letter-writer, particularly to his beloved younger sister and twin brothers, and his correspondence makes us privy to his emotional highs and lows, and to an endlessly fascinating picture of domestic trivia. His letters to von Meck, however, reveal him as a philosopher and a searcher for truth in his music.

He died in 1893, probably by suicide, although this has never been proved.

In recent years he has been much maligned over his life-style but his great-niece Galina von Meck (who was also the grand-daughter of his patron) probably made a fair assessment when she summed him up as 'the kind, considerate, very charming and humane member of our family'.

Right

Kamenka, the home of Tchaikovsky's sister and her husband, where Tchaikovsky spent many holidays. It was here in 1871 that he made The Lake of Swans *ballet for the Davidov children, and four years later composed some of the music for* Swan Lake

The Nineteenth Century

Towards the end of the nineteenth century Marius Petipa in St Petersburg was to take ballet on into a golden age, but for the first two-thirds of the century, ballet's capital was in Paris. It was there at the Opéra that the outstanding new works of the time were created, Filippo Taglioni's *La Sylphide* (1832), Jean Coralli and Jules Perrot's *Giselle* (1841) and Arthur Saint-Léon's *Coppélia* (1870), and the public flocked to see leading dancers of the day such as Marie Taglioni, Fanny Elssler, Carlotta Grisi, Fanny Cerrito and Lucile Grahn.

Ballet's Romantic age had arrived, slightly later than in art, literature and music, but proclaiming itself with just as much insistence. The public demanded escape into an enchanted realm, and so in ballet the period came to symbolize the setting up of mortals alongside supernatural creatures. Poetic lyricism assumed new meaning through *ballets blancs*, where women were seen, in the unearthly glow of pale moonlight, as idealized beauties in the form of sylphs, wilis, peris and naiads. Gradual transformation of style, as they began to rise *sur les pointes*, made it appear too as though they were hovering in flight. It was an age when the ballerina reigned supreme, and the leading male dancer was reduced in status until he became little more than a *porteur* and mime. Indeed, so unfashionable did he become that the hero of *Coppélia* was played by a pretty woman *en travestie*.

Such a state of affairs was all very well, but it was ridiculous to suppose that, in a world of continually changing values, men should continue in subsidiary roles. However, only one choreographer of note in the nineteenth century recognized the foolishness of such a sexual imbalance, and that was the Dane, August Bournonville, (1805–1879).

As a dancer he too had gone to Paris to study under the renowned Auguste Vestris, who also taught Perrot and Petipa and thus played a major role in shaping the foremost choreographers of the time, and by 1826 he had risen to the rank of soloist at the Opéra. It was afterwards, following his return to Copenhagen, that his real work began, with the creation of thirty-six ballets, and *divertissements*, in which male and female characters were assured of proper representation. His version of *La Sylphide* and *Napoli*, his most successful creations, remain internationally popular today.

He moulded the French style into what became known as the Bournonville school, concentrating on brilliant *terre à terre* work and spectacular *ballon*, set within phrases of continually changing speeds and directions. Petipa, too, when he went to Russia was to emphasize the French

Right
The Pas de Quatre, *choreographed by Jules Perrot to music by Pugni, and first performed at Her Majesty's Theatre, London 12 July 1845, with Marie Taglioni (centre) and (from right to left) Carlotta Grisi, Lucile Grahn and Fanny Cerito. The lithograph by T. H. Maguire from a drawing by A. E. Chalon is one of the most famous to have survived the Romantic period of ballet, and a version of the* Pas de Quatre, *with choreography by Anton Dolin, is still danced today*

Above
Marie Taglioni (1804–1884) in her most famous role, La Sylphide, choreographed by her father Filippo Taglioni (1778–1871)

influence, but he transformed it on to Russian bodies
capable of exceptional strength and pliancy, particularly in
the back, which meant that Russian ballet assumed a quite
different and distinctive look. He was aided by two teachers,
Christian Johansson, a Swede and former pupil of Bournonville's, and Enrico Cecchetti, an Italian virtuoso who had
trained in Florence under Giovanni Lepri (who himself
studied under the major codifier of classical training, Carlo

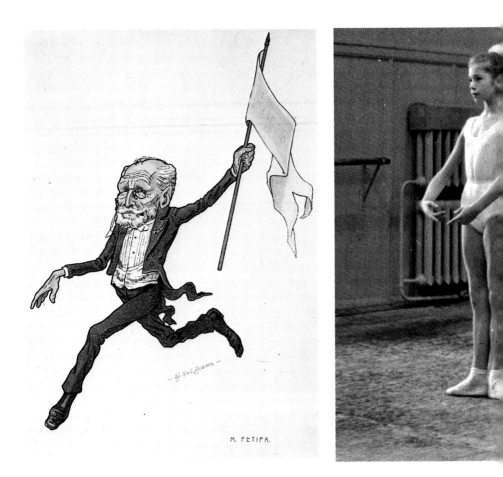

M. PETIPA.

Above

*Marius Petipa as depicted
by his colleague Nicholas
Legat, in one of a series of
cartoons published in his
book on the Russian ballet*

Blasis) and was to become one of the most important ballet
teachers of all time. In fact so valuable were the Bournonville, Russian and Cecchetti schools that even today they
continue to be associated with the highest standards.

Meanwhile, in nineteenth-century Russia there was no
call for the ballerina to share her pinnacle with her partner.
The pre-eminent ballet companies in Moscow and St
Petersburg each vied for superiority over the other, but when
in 1877 Moscow presented the first *Swan Lake*, the company
was at a low ebb. By then the man with the true gift of
leadership had settled in St Petersburg and was busy creating
La Bayadère, a work of lasting impact.

La Bayadère's score was written by the official composer
of the Imperial Theatres, Ludwig Minkus. But ballet music
then was not treated seriously by musicians, who ridiculed
composers such as Minkus and Cesare Pugni for producing

simple melody over firm rhythms which, though accessible enough to the ballet public, were in effect sweet and banal. How different the course of *Swan Lake* might have been if Tchaikovsky had remained in St Petersburg after graduating, and written his original score in consultation with Petipa.

The ballet master in those times had the upper hand, and Petipa was accustomed to issuing precise instructions to composers about style, time signatures and duration. Tchaikovsky responded to his requirements for *The Sleeping Beauty* and *The Nutcracker* in such a way that, far from thwarting his gifts, the imposed discipline seemed to inspire him still further. Nevertheless he was not averse to altering measures where it suited him, and he generally wrote more music than required.

Petipa was the most ordered of choreographers; he would plan his ballets meticulously before rehearsals began,

Above
Children of the Kirov ballet school, inheritors of the legacy left by Petipa

working at home from sketches, and copious notes, then using model figures in constructing patterns for his soloists and ensembles. Tchaikovsky was, of course, a master of symphonic structure and this is why today, however much compromise was effected between the two, we attach such importance to their collaboration.

Petipa's gifts were encouraged by growing up in a theatrical family, for his father Jean was an itinerant ballet master, and his mother a tragic actress, and they travelled wherever their work took them. He was born in Marseilles in 1818, but soon the family moved to Brussels where Petipa's father started giving Marius and his elder brother Lucien ballet lessons, and where Marius also began music studies at the Conservatoire.

He made rapid progress as a dancer and in his early teens gave his début performance. The family moved on to Antwerp, then Bordeaux, and at sixteen he was engaged as a soloist in Nantes, where he choreographed his first, short ballets. A visit to New York with his father, on an engagement that turned into a fiasco, sent him back to France, where he studied under Auguste Vestris. Lucien, who was himself to achieve a modest success as a choreographer, was *premier danseur* at the Opéra at the time, and in 1841 won a place in history when he appeared as Albrecht in the first performance of *Giselle*.

Petipa subsequently went as leading dancer to Bordeaux and then Madrid. He returned to Paris but could find no work. His travels, though, had exposed him to a wide range of experiences and choreographers, and soon he was to reveal just how deeply he had absorbed these influences and would use them to advantage in his own creations. His father by then was teaching in St Petersburg, and so it was presumably through Jean's intervention that Marius found himself accepting an invitation to go to that city as *premier danseur*, little knowing that he was to make his home there for the rest of his life, and that he was to be the last and greatest of a line of Frenchmen to lead the company almost throughout the nineteenth century. First of all, however, he had to serve his apprenticeship under Jules Perrot and Arthur Saint-Léon, and soon after his arrival in 1847 he found himself not only dancing but also staging existing ballets for the company.

In 1862 he had his first major success as a choreographer with *Pharaoh's Daughter*, which revealed his flair for creating full-length ballets à *grand spectacle*. This led to his appointment as second ballet master, but he still had to wait until 1870, and Saint-Léon's departure for France, before he

Arthur Saint-Léon (1821–1870) as Phoebus de Chateaupers in La Esmeralda *in a lithograph by J. Brandard. The ballet was choreographed by Jules Perrot to music by Pugni, with décor by William Grieve, and was first performed at Her Majesty's Theatre, London in 1844*

was given his head as ballet master-in-chief. His prede-
cessors had provided him with a sound foundation for his
craft, and taught him how to reveal drama through poetry
and link it into principal and secondary solos, as well as into
ensembles for classical and character dancers.

Even so, he was expected at first to conform and produce
ballets in the *féerie* style, in keeping with the public's
expectations. Visiting the city in 1874, Bournonville was
shocked by the absurdity of such ballets which, in their
eagerness to provide delights for the eyes rather than
stimulation for the mind, seemed empty and often vulgar. He
criticized them in his autobiography *My Theatre Life*, saying
that they were 'completely in conflict with my ideas about
the art of Terpsichore', and complained about them in
private to Petipa and Johansson, who agreed with him and
said that they 'loathed and despised this whole development', but were 'obliged to follow the current of the times
which they charged to the blasé (or conservative) taste of the
public and the specific wishes of the high authorities'.

Nevertheless, Petipa who, during his time in St Petersburg, was to produce a total of fifty-four new ballets, mount
seventeen revivals and create dances for some thirty-five
operas, gradually found his way out of the morass of bad
taste. He altered the focus so that form came to be as
important as content, and created fuller characters to help
reveal something of their emotional complexity.

Above
*Puss in Boots, one of the
fairy-tale characters from
the final act of* The Sleeping
Beauty. *An original design
for the production in 1890
at the Maryinsky Theatre*

He also took ballet on from Romanticism to its Classical
age, although the dividing line between the two is often
blurred, as with *Swan Lake* where the white acts herald a
Romantic ballet, whereas in overall form and design it is a
Classical ballet.

There can be no doubt that Petipa's crowning glory was
The Sleeping Beauty, the grandest dance spectacle ever
witnessed at the Maryinsky Theatre, which itself was
probably the most sumptuous theatre in the world. But the
extent of his achievement may be further realized in other
lasting ballets such as *Don Quixote*, the Kingdom of Shades
scene from *La Bayadère*, and in the Grand Pas both from
Paquita and *Raymonda*.

Petipa had a fondness for Russian dancers; he married two
of them, and his daughter Maria had a distinguished career
as a character dancer—even creating the mimed role of the
Lilac Fairy in *The Sleeping Beauty*. An unwritten law,
however, obliged him to cast Italian ballerinas, of whom
there was an influx in the city at the time, in the most
prominent roles. But he had cause to be grateful to them not
just for their interpretations—especially Carlotta Brianza in

The Sleeping Beauty, Antoinette Dell'Era in Ivanov's *Nutcracker* and Pierina Legnani in *Swan Lake*—but for the way their brilliance was assimilated into the Russian technique. For Petipa, despite his background, and even though he never mastered the language, had to all intents and purposes become a complete Russian.

Towards the end of his life he published his memoirs, but they are the reflections of a man who had grown embittered and who had gone on working beyond his peak, long after the time when he should have recognized the wisdom of retirement. His final ballet *The Magic Mirror* (1903) was a failure. He had been forced into producing it by the director at that time, Colonel Telyakovsky, despite the fact that he was unhappy about the music, and even unhappier about the designs, and the first performance was greeted with derisory hoots and catcalls. After that he was forced to step down, and the petty management forbade him entry behind the scenes at the Maryinsky, even though he had no obvious successor. In fact there was no one to lead the company on into the twentieth century until the emergence of Mikhail Fokine, who wanted to turn ballet upside-down with his reforms. But by 1909 Diaghilev was to lure Fokine away to his own company, and that move changed the entire course of ballet history.

Petipa died in 1908, convinced that he had been a failure. For a man who had rescued Russian ballet from its backwater and taken it to its apogee, it was a tragic final curtain.

Below
The Maryinsky Theatre, St Petersburg, renamed in 1935 the Kirov Theatre in Leningrad. Ballet performances were given originally in the city's Bolshoi Theatre but in 1886, under Ivan Vsevolojsky's directorship of the Imperial Theatres, they were transferred to the Maryinsky, where they have continued to this day

Lev Ivanov

The name Lev Ivanovich Ivanov is unlikely to mean anything to today's public even though, in the way of popular culture, many people who have never been to the ballet have vague notions about swan maidens grouped in graceful lines and lace-like patterns, in the tradition established by his choreography. He was a creator whose exceptional talents went largely unrecognized during his lifetime.

He was born in Moscow in 1834 and had a sad childhood in which he was shunted around by his mother between a foundling hospital and a merchant's family, before moving on to boarding-school. But when he was 10 years old he entered the Imperial School of Ballet at St Petersburg, and so began his association with the organization to which he was to devote the rest of his life.

While still very young he revealed what has been described as a phenomenal gift for music, and he is said to have been able to reproduce instantly on the piano any music he heard. Some years later a fellow dancer, Alexander Viktorovitch Shiryaev, recalled an occasion when 'Anton Grigorevich Rubinstein played through his ballet *The Grapevine* in the rehearsal hall. The composer had hardly left the hall before Ivanov sat down at the piano and reproduced practically all of Rubinstein's music by ear.' Rubinstein is said to have been as delighted as he was astonished. But though attempts were made in Ivanov's student days to lure him to the Conservatoire, he showed no enthusiasm for music study; and while he composed occasional pieces of music he never learnt the art of orchestration, or even how to commit his works to manuscript.

Above
Lev Ivanovich Ivanov caricatured by Nicholas Legat in his book on the Russian ballet

He joined the Imperial Ballet in 1852, under Jules Perrot, where he rose gradually to the level of principal dancer, performing for an exceptional forty years, and making his mark not so much as a *danseur noble* but as a mime, the creator of countless character roles. Ironically his gifts as a choreographer were reversed and realized not in mime, but in the creation of flowing dance.

After his first six years with the company he began also to teach at the school, and his subsequent career as teacher and coach among his colleagues blossomed until he was appointed first *régisseur* and then assistant ballet master under Petipa. His responsibilities were to revive existing ballets (and here too he revealed an exceptional gift of memory), and to create dances for the operas. In 1890 he choreographed the Polovtsian Dances for *Prince Igor* yet few people seemed to respond to their innate qualities. Later

Fokine had a palpable success with his ballet *Prince Igor* and Shiryaev recognized that this new ballet owed its inspiration to Ivanov's original dance patterns.

The problem was that Ivanov never escaped from under Petipa's wing. Had he done so it is possible that he might have left a larger dance legacy. Historians continue to evaluate his gifts, but point out that if the label 'genius' could properly be applied then he would surely somehow have found a way of letting his creative voice be heard continually, instead of only occasionally.

Perhaps it was his fault that laurels were not heaped upon him when, at the height of his powers, he choreographed *The Nutcracker* and the intensely poetic images of the lakeside scenes in *Swan Lake*, for he was said to be a shy and modest, though popular man. In her book *Era of the Russian Ballet* Natalia Roslaveva describes how she discovered that Ivanov was also 'to a considerable extent responsible for the poetic Vision Scene' in *The Sleeping Beauty*.

Ivanov married twice and had three children (one of whom was deaf and dumb) by each wife. But despite his dedication to work, he had a constant financial battle to support his family, and even at the end of his life he was forced to petition for money. When he died in 1901, not a single obituary made mention of *Swan Lake*, nor, strangely, had he referred to it in his own brief memoirs.

Above
Décor by Nicholai Roerich for Fokine's Polovtsian Dances from Prince Igor. *Ballets Russes, Paris 1909*

The Twentieth Century

Swan Lake, probably the most loved of all ballets, is today produced throughout the length and breadth of the ballet world. From China to Cuba, from Japan to Argentina, companies consider it crucial to their repertoire if credibility with the public is to be assured. For the dancers too it is a yardstick because it demands (or should demand) classical dancing of the highest calibre.

There have been hundreds of different productions in a never-ending line of revised thoughts on the subject, since each succeeding generation requires something more, whether from a need to present a heightened sense of tragedy or an extended form of allegory. The Petipa/Ivanov version is revered still, but while Ivanov's white acts are often incorporated into newer versions, Petipa's contributions have suffered more drastic changes. In any event, as Alicia Markova, who inherited her knowledge of the classics in a direct line from Diaghilev's company, and then as the first English Odette/Odile, has remarked, tiny alterations of nuance and phrasing have crept in over the years so that even when Petipa's choreography is said to be authentic, it is nowadays impossible to tell precisely how his creations are reproduced.

Nor is the music sacrosanct, for the score, whether in its 1877 or 1895 version, has undergone endless mutilations

Above
Anna Pavlova (1881–1931) and Nicholas Legat (1869–1937) in the lakeside scene from Swan Lake

and interpolations; but so deeply is it embedded in our culture that its most popular tunes are instantly recognized.

Some characters have vanished; others have been invented and later dismissed. Benno, Siegfried's companion, disappeared from many productions in the 1950s, but in Moscow in 1920 Alexander Gorsky, who made five different productions of the ballet, introduced a jester, principally to show off the brilliant talents of Vassily Yefimov. Since then, some producers have considered him to be essential to the ballet; but while he may be popular still in Russia, to Western audiences of today his antics can look coy and out of place.

The 1895 production lasted in St Petersburg until 1933 when, in the climate of change, Agrippina Vagananova (later a celebrated teacher) introduced a neo-realist version that achieved some notoriety, and included the Prince deciding to go hunting after his friends had confronted him with a dead swan.

In Soviet times the decree went out that, in keeping with the new idealism, the ballet should have a happy ending; and Russian productions have never progressed from their fondness for heavy melodrama. But these shortcomings can be forgiven if the quality of the dancing is superlative, as it generally is when seen in the West.

Below
Artists of the Australian Ballet in Anne Woolliam's 1977 production of Swan Lake

In England during 1910 the ballet was presented twice daily at the London Hippodrome as part of a music-hall programme given by twenty of 'Russia's acknowledged greatest dancers'; but since the production lasted an hour and went no further than Act II its impact was clearly limited. The following year in London Diaghilev presented a version at Covent Garden, based on Petipa/Ivanov but condensed into two acts. His choreographer was Fokine, and with men of such distinctive taste it might have been assumed that they would produce something of note. However, their adaptation contained some curious musical interpolations, with

The fiery temperaments of Rudolf Nureyev and Natalia Makarova matched in the Black Swan pas de deux. Both were members of the Kirov Ballet until their defection to the West (1961 and 1970 respectively) where each has contributed immeasurably to the art of dance

Vaslav Nijinsky dancing a solo to the Sugar Plum Fairy's music from *The Nutcracker*, and Mathilde Kschessinskaya appearing in a solo to music composed by Kadletz, and the first audiences were bored by it.

London, nevertheless, is important in the history of *Swan Lake*, for in 1934 the Vic-Wells (now Royal) Ballet presented the first full-length version of the Petipa/Ivanov production ever to be given outside Russia. It was staged by Nicolai Sergeyev, the former St Petersburg *régisseur* who had escaped from Russia in 1918 together with his notes on the company's turn-of-the century repertoire, meticulously copied into Stepanov notation (a form of ballet shorthand).

Although the Vic-Wells company was young, and the production consequently modest, the West had inherited a priceless treasure. Three years later Margot Fonteyn made her début as Odette/Odile with the company, and from then until relatively recently, she was to be hailed as one of the ballet's greatest interpreters. Indeed, by 1969 Clive Barnes was reviewing a performance for the *New York Times* and claiming that 'she has danced more performances of this role than any other ballerina anywhere'. He went on to describe the occasion saying that emotionally she 'expressed precisely that curious Tchaikovsky lament of the swan—that image of romanticism remote from reality, yet still real enough to die for. Fonteyn's Odette is all frozen pain and coldly crystallized understanding.'

Alicia Markova and Robert Helpmann in Act II, Vic-Wells Ballet. Produced by Markova and Anton Dolin, the lakeside act was first presented on its own in 1932. This photograph was taken in 1934 soon after the young Margot Fonteyn had joined the corps de ballet. *She is standing second in line in the front row*

Her regular partner by then was Rudolf Nureyev. Five years earlier in Vienna their performances, in a production of the ballet by Nureyev himself, had won them a place in the *Guinness Book of Records* following a remarkable 89 curtain calls. It was a partnership that saw the fusion of the Russian and British schools into a single and unique entity.

Nureyev had moved on from the Soviet ideology of his youth, his thinking reflected in an increased sense of drama and tragedy and in ways of wresting the Prince from his passive role to one with more substance and character. His conception was perhaps an extension of the new choreography he introduced into Robert Helpmann's Royal Ballet production of 1963, which included the Prince's solo of yearning lines and contemplative poses at the end of Act I. Emotionally it made such good sense that many subsequent choreographers have considered that it belonged to the ballet by right. In another notable version of the 1960s made for the Stuttgart Ballet, John Cranko showed that he too was working on similar lines, and that the tragedy inherent in Tchaikovsky's music had to be brought out.

Two choreographers who chose to go back, so far as was possible, to the 1877 score, were Vladimir Bourmeister in Moscow in 1953, and Jack Carter a decade later in Buenos Aires in a production that he subsequently mounted for London Festival Ballet. Both felt instinctively that they should follow the composer in his original thoughts, and both introduced prologues in which Odette first appeared among girls collecting flowers and was then metamorphosed by von Rothbart into a swan.

Peter Darrell's production for Scottish Ballet also used the original score in celebration of its centenary but the scenario was far from traditional. His Siegfried was an opium-smoking prince, who envisaged Odile as idealized love (Odette) in an hallucinatory dream.

In Canada Erik Bruhn created a controversial adaptation for the National Ballet in which he reverted to an earlier form of the legend presenting von Rothbart as a woman—an enigmatic Black Queen.

Even George Balanchine, who deliberately turned his back on old-style classicism, was tempted by Tchaikovsky's music, making in 1951 an idiomatic one-act version of the ballet for New York City Ballet.

The Royal Ballet has continued to present new productions, roughly one every decade, gradually incorporating newer choreography, notably by Frederick Ashton. The Sadler's Wells Royal Ballet, its sister company, also represented a spectacular new version in 1981 by Peter Wright

One of the most memorable interpretations of the 1960s was the production by John Cranko for the Stuttgart Ballet. In it he stressed the ballet's dramatic intensity, declaring that Siegfried 'is a tragic hero and must be vanquished. The tone of the music, especially in the fourth act, is tragic . . . Odette and Siegfried are not the sort of lovers who can live happily ever after.' Lucia Isenring Montagon and Egon Madsen are seen here in Act IV

and Galina Samsova which, perhaps for the first time, made reference to the Prince's ignored father by opening with his funeral procession. This gave added relevance to the Queen Mother's concern for her son's marriage by linking it to the question of royal succession.

Another production in the 1980s by Nureyev, this time for the Paris Opéra, revealed Odile and von Rothbart as the reversed images of Odette and Wolfgang. Also in this decade we find a fashion for presenting *Swan Lake* without its swans, stressing that between midnight and dawn the beautiful creatures beside the lake were allowed to be maidens, and had no need to take on the image of swans. The idea was tempting enough to lure Franco Zeffirelli away from his more regular position as an opera producer to make his own production for the ballet company of La Scala, Milan.

And so *Swan Lake* goes on, through all its enduring traditions and rebellions. At worst new audiences may be left wondering what all the fuss is about, but at best they may find something of what Tchaikovsky described when talking of his work in a letter to his patron Mme von Meck: 'It is a musical confession of the soul, which is full to the brim and which, turned to its essential nature, pours itself out in sound, just as the lyric poet expresses himself in verse. The difference is that music possesses incomparably more powerful means and is a subtler language for the articulation of the thousand different moments of the soul's moods.'

Above
Natalia Makarova and Anthony Dowell gliding to eternity in the Royal Ballet's 1977 production

Eva Evdokimova in Beryl Grey's 1972 production for London Festival Ballet. Although Evdokimova was born in Geneva and first danced professionally with the Royal Danish Ballet, she has since become a guest star of international standing and one who excels in romantic roles

Index

Ashton, Frederick 46

Balanchine, George 44
Ballet of La Scala, Milan 46
Ballet of the Paris Opéra 46
Barnes, Clive 43
La Bayadère 32, 36
Beaumont, Cyril 12
Begichev, Vladimir
  Petrovich 13, 14
Bellini, Vincenzo 26
Blasis, Carlo 31, 32
Bocharov, Mikhail Ilyich 23
Bourmeister, Vladimir 44
Bournonville, August 30,
  34
Brianza, Carlotta 37
Bruhn, Erik 44

Carter, Jack 44
Cecchetti, Enrico 31
Cerrito, Fanny 30
Cinderella 14
Coppélia 30
Coralli, Jean 30
Cranko, John 44

Darrell, Peter 44
Davydov, Yuri Lvovich 12
Delibes, Léo 15
Dell'Era, Antoinette 37
Diaghilev, Serge 37, 40, 42
Don Giovanni 26
Don Quixote 36
Donizetti, Gaetano 26
Drigo, Riccardo 21
Dürbach, Fanny 26

Elssler, Fanny 30
Eugene Onegin 14

Fokine, Mikhail 36, 39, 42
Fonteyn, Margot 43

Geltser, Vasily Fedorovich
  13
Gerdt, Pavel 23

Gillert, Stanislav 18
Giselle 30, 34
Gorsky, Alexander 40
Grahn, Lucile 30
Grisi, Carlotta 30

Hansen, Joseph 19
Helpmann, Robert 44

Ivanov, Lev Ivanovich 18,
  20, 37, 38, 39, 40, 42, 43

Jacobi, Georges 19
Johansson, Christian 31, 36

Karpakova, Pelagia
  Mikhailovna 18
Kschessinskaya, Mathilde
  43

Laroche, Herman
  Avgustovich 24, 26–7
Legnani, Pierina 23, 37
Lepri, Giovanni 31
Lohengrin 15
London Festival Ballet 44

Markova, Alicia 40
Meck, Galina von 28
Meck, Nadezhda von 26,
  28, 46
Meck-Davydov, Anna 12,
  15
Minkus, Ludwig 19, 32

Napoli 30
The National Ballet of
  Canada 44
New York City Ballet 44
Nijinsky, Vaslav 43
Nuryev, Rudolf 44, 46
The Nutcracker 20, 33, 37,
  39, 43

Paquita 36
Petipa, Jean 34
Petipa, Lucien 34

Petipa, Maria 36
Petipa, Marius 18, 20, 23,
  30, 33, 34, 36, 37, 38,
  39, 40, 42, 43
Perrault, Charles 20
Perrot, Jules 30, 34, 36
Pharaoh's Daughter 34
Polovtsian Dances 38
Prince Igor 38, 39
Pugni, Cesare 32

Raymonda 36
Reisinger, Julius 16
Rimsky-Korsakov, Nikolai
  Andreyevich 15
Roslaveva, Natalia 39
Rossini, Gioacchino 26
The Royal Ballet 43, 44
Rubinstein, Anton
  Grigorevich 38

Sadler's Wells Royal Ballet
  46
Saint-Léon, Arthur 30, 34
Samsova, Galina 46
Sergeyev, Nicolai 43
Shilovskaya, Marya
  Vasilevna 14
Shilovsky, Konstantin 14
Shilovsky, Vladimir 13, 15
Shiryaev, Alexander
  Viktorovitch 38, 39
The Sleeping Beauty 20, 33,
  36, 37, 39
Slonimsky, Yuri 12
Sobeshchanskaya, Anna
  Iosifovna 18
The Swans 19
The Stuttgart Ballet 44
La Sylphide (Bournonville)
  30
La Sylphide (Taglioni) 30
Sylvia 15

Taglioni, Filippo 30
Taglioni, Marie 30
Tchaikovsky, Anatoli 15

Tchaikovsky, Modeste
  Ilyich 12, 16
Tchaikovsky, Peter Ilyich 6,
  12, 13, 14, 15, 16, 19,
  20, 23, 24–8, 33, 34, 43,
  44, 46
Telyakovsky, Vladimir
  Arkadievich 37

Undine 27

Vaganova, Agrippina 40
Valts, Karl 16
Vestris, Auguste 30, 34
Vic-Wells Ballet, see Royal
  Ballet
The Voyevoda 26, 27
Vsevolojsky, Ivan
  Alexandrovich 20

Wagner, Richard 15
Wiley, Roland John 19, 21
Wright, Peter 46

Yefimov, Vassily 40

Zeffirelli, Franco 46

Acknowledgments
The Australian Ballet Foundation 40–1;
Bibliothèque Nationale 17; Covent Garden
Archives 15; The Dancing Times 33; Zoe
Dominic 42; E.T. Archive 25, 27, 31, 35, 39;
London Festival Ballet/Mike Davis 6–7, 18, 22;
/Zoe Dominic 47; Robert Harding Picture Library
36; Novosti 8–9, 12–13, 16, 22, 24, 29; Royal
Ballet Benevolent Fund 11; Society for Cultural
Relations with the USSR 28; Leslie Spatt 45;
Theatre Museum 43; Victoria and Albert
Museum 14, 15, 30; Reg Wilson 18–19, 46